How SUBMARINES Work

By Mary Hertz Scarbrough

MODERN CURRICULUM PRESS

Pearson Learning Group

The following people from Pearson Learning Group have contributed to the development of this product:

Art and Design: Dorothea Fox, Jennifer Ribnicky

Editorial: Leslie Feierstone Barna, Nicole Iorio, Jennie Rakos

Inventory: Levon Carter

Marketing: Alison Bruno

Production: Roxanne Knoll

All photography © Pearson Education, Inc. (PEI) unless otherwise specifically noted.

Photographs: Cover: *t* © Metacreations/Kai Power Photos, *b* © Barry Lewis/Alamy; 5: © Picture Desk, Inc./Kobal Collection; 8–9: © Science Museum; 10: © Steve Kaufman /AGE Fotostock; 14–15: © Michael Melford/The Image Bank/Getty Images. Illustration: 6: Christine Schneider.

QuickReads®, Modern Curriculum Press®, Developmental Reading Assessment®, and the DRA logo are trademarks, in the U.S. and/or in other countries, of Pearson Education, Inc. or its affiliate(s).

Lexile is a U.S. registered trademark of MetaMetrics, Inc. All rights reserved.

ISBN-13: 978-1-4284-1240-8
ISBN-10:　　1-4284-1240-9

Printed in the United States of America
1 2 3 4 5 6 7 8 9 10 11 10 09 08 07

Modern
Curriculum
Press

Pearson Learning Group

1-800-321-3106
www.pearsonlearning.com

Contents

All About Submarines

Deep under the **ocean** water, a kind of ship moves. Other ships can only sail on the **surface** of the water. This ship can **travel** both under water and on the surface of the ocean. This kind of ship is a **submarine**.

The first submarines were made in the 1600s. A crew of 12 people gave the first submarine its power. The crew had to use **oars** to travel. The oars came out of holes on the sides of the submarine. Water could not get in the holes where the oars were. The crew could stay under water for a few hours. Air came in through a tube above the surface of the water. The submarine could only go about 12 feet below the surface.

Another of the first submarines was called the Turtle. It looked like a turtle. The Turtle's power came from one person hard at work using both hands to turn two cranks.

This picture has the side cut out to show what it looks like in the Turtle.

shut to keep
air in

tank full
of air

Air in the submarine's tanks makes the submarine float. As the
tanks fill with water, the submarine goes below the surface.

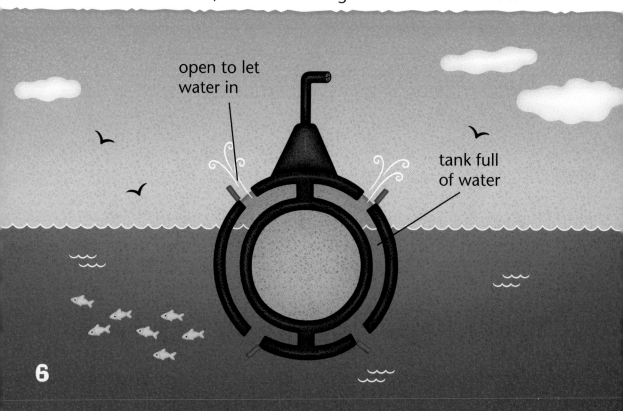

open to let
water in

tank full
of water

Turning one of the Turtle's cranks made the submarine move across the water. Turning the other crank made the submarine move up in the water. The Turtle was the first submarine used in a war. This war began in 1775.

How A Submarine Works

A submarine has tanks. These tanks are full of air when the submarine floats on the surface. When the tanks fill with water, the submarine goes below the surface, or sinks.

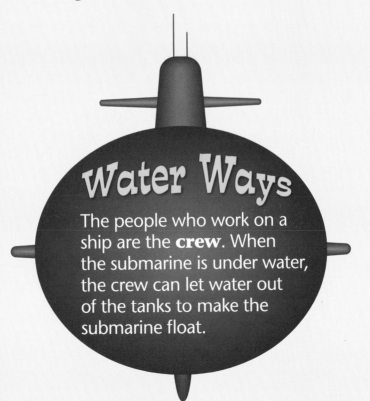

Water Ways

The people who work on a ship are the **crew**. When the submarine is under water, the crew can let water out of the tanks to make the submarine float.

Better Submarines

In about 1900 the first submarine with an **engine** was made. The engine was in the ship to give it power. With an engine, the crew did not have to do all the work that people used to do. The submarine could travel without oars or cranks. People learned how to make engines safe. In the last 100 years, submarines have been used for many different things.

This is what a submarine from about 100 years ago looked like.

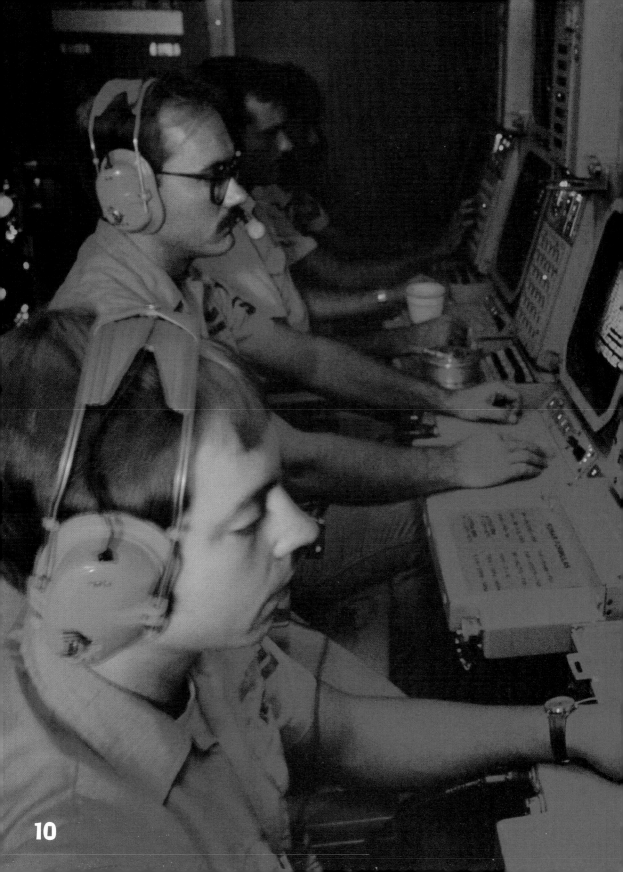

Submarine travel helps us learn about animals and plants that live deep in the ocean. We can even travel in submarines for fun. Today's submarines still use tanks with water and air to go up and down in the water.

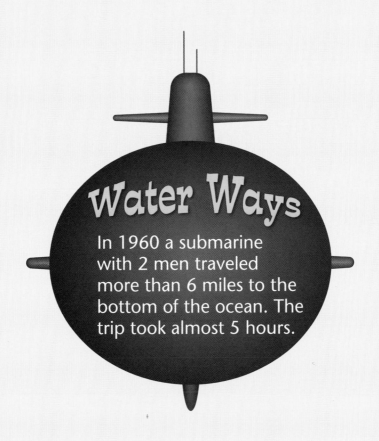

Water Ways

In 1960 a submarine with 2 men traveled more than 6 miles to the bottom of the ocean. The trip took almost 5 hours.

These people are hard at work in a submarine.

Floating Marbles

Try an **experiment** that shows you how a submarine works. You will need **marbles**, a small jar with a lid, and a tub of water. Put the lid on the jar, and put the jar in the water.

What do you see? Does the jar float? Use a smaller jar if the jar starts to sink or sinks to the bottom.

Next, put a marble into the jar. Close the lid to keep water out. Put the jar into the water. The jar should still float.

Put more marbles into the jar. See how many marbles you need to make the jar start to sink. How many marbles do you need to make the jar hit the bottom?

A jar full of air floats in water. Adding marbles to the jar makes the jar sink.

The jar with marbles in it is like a submarine below the surface. Adding marbles in this experiment is like adding water to the ship's tanks. In the experiment the jar that floats is like a submarine that floats on the ocean. The jar floats when it is full of air. A submarine floats when its tanks are full of air.

Water Ways

The water in a submarine's tanks could fill several big pools.

Tanks full of air make submarines like this one float on the surface of the water.

Glossary

crew people who work on a submarine

engine the part of a submarine that helps it move

experiment a way to see how something works

marbles small, glass balls

oars things used to move a submarine

ocean a large body of water

submarine a ship that can travel on the surface of the water and below the surface of the water

surface the top or outer level

travel to go from one place to another place

INSIDE THE Amazon Rain Forest

By Jaime Joyce

MODERN CURRICULUM PRESS

Pearson Learning Group

The following people from Pearson Learning Group have contributed to the development of this product:

Art and Design: Dorothea Fox, Jennifer Ribnicky

Editorial: Leslie Feierstone Barna, Nicole Iorio, Patricia Peters

Inventory: Levon Carter

Marketing: Alison Bruno

Production: Roxanne Knoll

All photography © Pearson Education, Inc. (PEI) unless otherwise specifically noted.

Photographs: Cover: © National Geographic Image Collection; 7: © Dr. Moreley Read/Science Photo Library/Photo Researchers, Inc.; 8: © Pete Oxford/Minden Pictures; 10–11: © Tui De Roy/Minden Pictures; 12: © Mark Bowler Amazon-Images/Alamy; 14–15: © Gerry Ellis/Minden Pictures; 16: © Luiz Claudio Marigo/Nature Picture Library; 18: © Frans Lanting/Minden Pictures; 21: © ZSSD/Minden Pictures; 22–23: © Peter Oxford/Nature Picture Library. Illustrations: 4–5: Pamela Johnson.

ISBN-13: 978-1-4284-1242-2

ISBN-10:   1-4284-1242-5

Printed in the United States of America
1 2 3 4 5 6 7 8 9 10   11 10 09 08 07

Modern Curriculum Press

Pearson Learning Group

1-800-321-3106
www.pearsonlearning.com

Contents

kapok tree

harpy eagle

bazil nut tree

kapok tree

fig

monkeys

tree boa

palm tree

bats

sloth

jaguar

dart frog

4

The Amazon

The sun begins to rise above the Amazon rain forest. Tall, green trees soak up the sun. It is warm and bright. Later, it will rain. Some animals that live in the trees below are just waking up. For others, it is time to go to sleep. It is a brand new day in the Amazon rain forest.

The Amazon rain forest is in South America. It is the biggest rain forest in the world. It spreads across about 2.5 million square miles. That is more than half the size of the United States!

Scientists found that the rain forest has four separate **layers**. The four layers are the **emergent** layer, the **canopy**, the **understory**, and the forest floor. Each layer of the Amazon rain forest is filled with different plants and animals.

Emergent

Canopy

Understory

Forest Floor

Rain forests have four different layers.

Life at the Top

To reach the emergent, or top, layer of the Amazon rain forest, trees need to be about 200 feet tall. That is as big as a 20-story building! Trees that grow this tall have thick trunks and thick roots. The trees' thick trunks and roots help keep the trees from blowing over in the strong winds. The emergent layer is also home to many birds.

Standing Tall

One of the tallest trees in the Amazon rain forest is the kapok tree. Kapok trees can grow to 200 feet tall. Their leaves are long and thin. Small, white flowers with a strong smell grow on the tree. These flowers smell bad to people but smell good to animals such as bats.

The trunk of the kapok tree is long, straight, and very thick. The trunks of some kapok trees are about 9 feet around. Others are even bigger. It would take at least three people holding hands to wrap around the trunk of a kapok tree. This tree is a good place for some animals to build their homes.

Kapok trees are some of the tallest trees in the rain forest.

A Big Bird

High in the sky above the emergent layer, a kind of eagle called a harpy spreads its wings. It flies over the top of a kapok tree. Then the harpy eagle swoops down into the rain forest for dinner. This eagle has spotted a monkey in the tree branches. The harpy eagle is a bird of **prey**. Birds of prey eat other animals. A monkey is prey, or food, for the eagle.

The harpy eagle is one of the animals that lives in the emergent layer of the Amazon rain forest. Harpy eagles build their nests in the tallest trees, and they are some of the biggest birds in the world. They weigh as much as 20 pounds and can grow to be about 3 feet tall. That is about as tall as a child who is two years old. The eagles can spread their wings out to 7 feet across. Most people cannot spread their arms that far!

Harpy eagles have gray feathers on their heads. The feathers sometimes stand up like a fan. The eagles have white feathers on their chests and legs. Black feathers cover the rest of their bodies.

A harpy eagle stands on a branch high up in a tree.

Harpy eagles hunt very well. They hide in the tree tops to watch their prey. Then they swoop down on animals such as monkeys. Their yellow feet have sharp claws that help them catch their prey. Their claws are as big as bear claws. After the eagle catches an animal, the harpy eagle takes its prey back to its nest to eat it.

Rain Forest Fact

The seeds of the kapok tree are filled with a material that is like cotton. This cotton material is used to fill life vests and beds.

The harpy eagle has very big claws.

Under the Roof

From above, the rain forest looks like a huge green sea. Sun beats down on the tops of the trees. Yet, below the trees, the light is dim. The sun cannot shine through the thick layer of trees that is just below the emergent layer. This layer is known as the canopy. The canopy is the main layer of the rain forest.

A canopy is a cover that **protects** things below it. The trees in the canopy protect the plants and animals in the layers below from the sun. After it rains, it stays wet under the canopy. Some plants need this water in the canopy. The canopy also gives animals places to hide from hungry animals.

The Amazon rain forest spreads for miles and miles, and it has many rivers.

Trees in the Canopy Layer

In the canopy, the trees are close together. Their branches touch the trees on either side of them. Vines hang down from the branches. This layer of the Amazon rain forest has the most fruits and nuts. The canopy is also home to more animal **species**, or types, than the other layers.

One of the trees in the canopy is the Brazil nut tree. Like the other trees in the canopy, the Brazil nut tree grows to about 150 feet tall. Inside the hard fruits on its branches, there can be as many as 24 huge seeds. These seeds are called Brazil nuts. Each Brazil nut is about an inch long. Many animals in the rain forest like to eat the nuts. People eat these nuts, too.

One kind of fig tree in the canopy is not like other trees. It starts out as a vine that grows in the branches of other trees. Soon, the vine gets bigger. Its roots hang down from the branches of the tree. Finally, the roots of the vine reach the forest floor. Then, the fig tree wraps itself around the trunk of the larger tree. Over time, the fig tree kills the tree that it grew on. When the tree has died, the fig tree is all that is left.

An Animal in Slow Motion

The sloth is a strange animal. It lives in the canopy of the rain forest. The sloth is the slowest **mammal** in the world. The sloth is so slow that green **algae** grow on its fur. Algae are a type of plant-like living things. The algae help to protect the sloth. The green algae help the sloth blend in with the green tree leaves in the canopy. This is important because the sloth is not fast enough to get away from animals that hunt it. The sloth stays safe by blending in with the canopy.

The sloth has a body that is made to live in trees. Its long claws help the sloth grab onto branches. The sloth also sleeps about 20 hours a day in the trees. When it is not sleeping, the sloth is eating. At night, the sloth eats tree leaves.

A sloth's long claws help it climb trees.

This monkey is using its long, strong tail to hang from a tree.

What a Monkey!

Monkeys also live in the canopy of the Amazon rain forest. Just like sloths, monkeys are mammals. One type of monkey has very long arms and legs that help it swing from the tree branches. It uses its tail like another arm. The monkey wraps its strong tail around tree branches and hangs upside down. The monkey's long tail helps it swing quickly from tree to tree.

At night, these monkeys sleep in branches in the tops of trees. They stay safe from hungry animals on the forest floor. During the day, the monkeys look for food. They eat fruit, nuts, tree leaves, and sometimes eggs from birds' nests.

Mean and Green

Monkeys do not eat snakes, but some snakes eat monkeys. One type of tree boa is a snake that eats monkeys. Like the monkey, the tree boa lives in the canopy of the Amazon rain forest. This snake is bright green. It wraps its body around tree branches. Its bright green color helps it blend in with the leaves and hide from other animals. Tree boas can grow to be 9 feet long. Tree boas use their sharp teeth to bite their prey. They also wrap their bodies around an animal until it cannot get air. The snakes can eat the animal whole!

Rain Forest Fact

There are so many trees and leaves in the canopy that they block most of the sunlight. Only about 2 percent of sunlight reaches the forest floor.

Made in the Shade

The understory layer of the rain forest is dark, hot, and damp. This layer is closer to the ground. The trees in the canopy above trap the heat and wet air. They also block the light.

Palm Tree Seeds

Palm trees grow in the understory. Like other plants in the understory, these trees do not need a lot of light. They have long, wide, green leaves to trap and store sunlight. Some palm trees grow fruit, which is its seeds. People crack open the seed's hard shell. This fruit has a drink inside.

Amazon palm trees live in the hot, damp understory of the rain forest.

A Fast Cat

The jaguar is one of the world's biggest cats. It is also found in the understory of the Amazon rain forest. The jaguar hides in the trees. It hunts by watching the forest floor. The jaguar looks and waits for animals to pass by. Then it jumps out of the tree to catch and eat its prey.

Fresh Blood Wanted

Bats also live in the understory. Bats are the only mammals that can fly. Like the jaguar, one type of bat watches from the darkness and waits for animals that live on the forest floor. These bats swoop down and sink their sharp teeth into their prey. These bats only eat fresh blood.

Rain Forest Fact

Some people who live in the Amazon rain forest use palm tree leaves from the understory to make roofs for their homes.

What Lies Below

It is dark and hot on the Amazon rain forest floor. Few plants can grow here because there is not enough light. Yet, there are some plants that grow best in places that are damp and dark. Ferns are plants that do grow well on the rain forest floor. They do not grow well in the sun.

One animal that lives in this layer of the Amazon rain forest is the **poison** dart frog. Poison dart frogs are bright colors, such as blue, red, and yellow. These tiny frogs are only about 2 inches long. However, the poison inside the frog's bodies can kill people and animals with a touch of its skin.

Rain Forest Fact

Some animals in the Amazon rain forest find interesting homes. Poison dart frogs sometimes live inside cracked Brazil nut pods. They even lay eggs in the pods.

Poison dart frogs live on the Amazon rain forest floor.

The Living Forest

The Amazon rain forest is like no other place in the world. Each of its four layers is home to many kinds of plants and animals. There are more plants and animals than scientists can count.

The Amazon rain forest is home to about 20 percent of the plants and birds found on Earth. It is also home to about 10 percent of the mammals that live on Earth. That is just the beginning. New species are discovered all the time that live under this natural roof of leaves—the Amazon rain forest.

Many species of birds live in the Amazon rain forest.

Glossary

algae type of plant-like living things

canopy a covering; the layer of the rain forest below the emergent layer

emergent growing out of; the top layer of the rain forest

layers levels

mammal an animal with warm blood that is usually covered with fur

poison something that harms or kills

prey an animal that another animal hunts for food

protects keeps safe

species type of animal or plant

understory the layer of the rain forest below the canopy